West Quoddy Lighthouse
By C.la. Macmillan

Part of the Proceeds from this Booklet will go to
West Quoddy Lighthouse Programs.

The West Quoddy Lighthouse
Perches on the Easternmost Point of land in
The United States
44 deg. 48.9 min. North Latitude
66 deg. 57.1 min. West Longitude

The Name Quoddy comes from Passamaquoddy
Reservation Name.

Congress appropriated $5000 for the light station on April 21, 1806. The contractors Beal and Thaxter built the first wooden lighthouse on the site, along with a small dwelling, in 1808. It was the first American lighthouse east of Penobscot Bay

Tower No. 1: Light station established on 21 April 1808 at a cost of $5,000. (Picture below)

Wood was the 3rd most common building material used in Lighthouse Construction., until funds were available to

build a more durable structure of Masonry or iron. In some locations, however, the wood tower remained or was chosen as the permanent lighthouse structure.

Easily shaped by sawing, planning, carving and gouging, wood was used for virtually all components of historic lighthouse. Wooden towers

were generally timber frame construction covered with sheathing and clapboards or shingles all other lighthouse components such as doors, windows, cornices, deck railings and decking were also constructed of wood.

Whale oil was used with solid wicks as the source of light until a parabolic reflector system was introduced around 1810. Although the Fresnel lens was invented in 1822, it wasn't used in this country until the 1850's. Reliable fog signal was deemed more essential in this area than a light source, since fog surrounded the coast for roughly half the time during the summer months and still does.

* 1st Keeper: Thomas Dexter served from 1808 to 1813 Salary $250.00

In 1813 Dexter Resigned, his closing inventory at the Station included as follows:

5~ Blank forms of Annual Returns & one filled up for Direction

8~ Ditto for Quarterly Accounts, Including Duplicates

1~ W.Lewis Book: Instruction to Manage for Light House

1~ Light House Dimensions as per Annual Return

1 ~Dwelling House... Wanting/Needing Repairs

1~ Oil Vault Containing 5 Oil Butts or Tubs Unoccupied (out of Repair)

1~ Small Row Boat- Much out of Repair having Neither Oars, Painted or Sails

1~ Hoisting Machine with 2 Block & Tackle Full- Wanting Hooks & Thimbles

The Note as Follows:

"There is not more than 10 days oil in the Vault, the British Commandant at Eastport claims the Control of the Lighthouse until the British Troops leave Coastline, also that he had been promised by the said Commandant that his Salary should be paid by the British Government & had received orders for his pay. To the 1st of the present month, and that being very poor & large family to support he ask liberty to draw on the Superintendent for his salary & hopes considering his situation the Government of the United States will indulge him in allowing him a part of his pay. Signed by Dexter, Thomas & Dated Mar. 5, 1813

*The 2nd Keeper: Peter Godfrey, 1813-39

Salary: Unknown

Who ran into difficulties also during the War of 1812. On April 8, 1815. History suggests that a British Commandant claimed control of West Quoddy Light Station during The Year of 1815. By the 1830's, all of the wooden lighthouses built by Benjamin Beal & Duncan W. Thaxter had deteriorated so much that they had to be replaced Because Wooden Towers burned, no Early Example Survive. Congress approved funds in March of 1831 for a replacement. Joseph Berry subsequently completed a rubble stone tower for $2,350, and the ten lamps in its lantern room were lit on August 1, 1831. Measuring 49 feet tall, West Quoddy wasn't the largest lighthouse in the country, but, it was greatly needed.

1820: On May 15, Congress authorizes the first fog signal, a 500-pound (bell), at the station for a cost of $1,000.

The Keeper. Was given an additional $60.00 annually, for Ringing the Bell .This Bell was replaced by 2nd Bell weighting 241 pounds that was said to have a more penetrating, high-pitched sound.

Then again this Bell was replaced by a 3rd Bell weighting 1,545 lbs. and Once again being replaced by the 4th Bell made of cast-steel "Capt. Joseph. Smith" said that This 4th Bell is" Worse than Useless"

Capt. Smith did recommend a light & bell to be place on Sail Rock (Photo below). 500 ft. off shore. In 1838 Congress Did Authorized funds for Light and bell on Sail rock. "This was never built"

This 2nd Masonry Tower 1831-1858 (see Picture) Congress appropriated $8000, and the contractor Joseph Berry rebuilt the tower in 1831 for $2350. The new rubblestone lighthouse, 49 feet tall, went into service on August 1, 1831 rubblestone split from the adjacent ledges or Cliffs or collected on the Beach were used to build the 2nd Tower. Some of the Stones are still visible on the Grounds of the West Quoddy Park today. The cracks between the Stones were filled with a lime and sand

Mortar. The walls were usually three feet thick at the Base, tapering to Two feet in Thickness at the Top. A brick dome was placed on the top of the tower and an Iron & Glass Lantern was attached to the Tower by imbedding the lower ends of its Iron Angle-Post into the Masonry walls

Ships would approached the bold coast in foggy conditions they would fire a gun signal to prompt the lighthouse keeper to start tolling the fog bell.

Just over a decade later, Keeper Alfred Godfrey, who succeeded his father after the latter's 26 years of service at the station, described the sorry condition of the dwelling and lighthouse at West Quoddy: "The house leaks all about the eaves and windows in rainy weather. The chimneys smoke badly...we have no rain water cistern, no well. Our water for domestic use is obtained from a spring about 200 yards from the house. The lighthouse stands 110 feet from my house door; on the edge of the cliff...The tower is built of rubble stone, badly laid. In winter the walls are coated with ice from the effect of leakage. The windows of the tower blow inward in storms from being insufficiently framed...In winter the inside of the glass is coated with ice, from the condensed vapors of the burning lamps, and in summer the glass is also covered with sweat and condensed vapor."

The 3rd Brick Lighthouse:. 1858 – Present (photo next Page)

On August 18, 1856, $15,000 was appropriated "for rebuilding the light-house," at West Quoddy Head, "and fitting it with proper illuminating apparatus." In this case, the "proper illuminating apparatus" was a fixed, third-order Fresnel lens manufactured by L. Sautter of Paris. The new brick tower and wood-framed dwelling, which remain standing today, were completed in 1858.

This new lighthouse brought some much needed conveniences; a Victorian style house for the keeper and his family By 1869 The first lighthouses to be regularly equipped with steam whistles was West Quoddy Head .Also The 2nd Building consisted of a boiler sometime later a Locomotive type whistle, giving each minute a blast of eight seconds duration, being the most powerful type of fog signal devised. With all the cannons, bells and trumpets going off all the time it's a wonder that anyone living at or near the light kept their hearing and their sanity. . Kerosene started replacing lard oil in the 1870's and the service was finally totally converted by the late 1880's. The quality of the light depended upon how well the wick was trimmed. Gradually, keepers were nicknamed "wickies." Electricity started to replace kerosene around the turn of the century.

FACTS:

Tower: 49 feet high (15 meters)

Diameter at base: 16 feet (4.88 meters),

Diameter at top: 14 feet (4.27 meters)

Tower Construction: Red Brick.

Center of Lantern 83 feet above sea level (25.3 meters)

Two ~ 1000 watt bulbs, 30,000 candle Power

Visible 15-18 miles (24-29 kilometers) at sea. Light flashes **(does not revolve)** 24 hours per day, in this sequence: 2 seconds on, 2 seconds off, 2 seconds on, 9 seconds off. The Copper Dome was

Replaced in 2004.

Notice the Gargoyles on the Dome. Architects often used multiple gargoyles on buildings to divide the flow of rainwater off the roof to minimize the potential damage from a rainstorm.

The Tower and Keeper's House prior to 1890s renovation remain the same, except the brick workroom is no longer connected to the house. The first 32 feet of the tower are common red brick. Eight red stripes alternate with seven white stripes. The stripes are about 25 inches wide. The bottom stripe and the top stripe are red. The tower has two windows of glass brick on the east side (facing the sea). These windows are about 40 inches wide and 30 inches wide. The lower window starts at the top of the first white stripe. The upper window starts at the top of the sixth white stripe.

Today this dramatic past is kept alive by the West Quoddy Head Lighthouse Keeper's Association whose visitor center is in the old keeper's house. Learn about the life of a lighthouse keeper by viewing exhibits of old photographs, uniforms and more donated by keepers and their families.

Visitors to the lighthouse can step back into the keeper's lonely life, which in early years was not an easy one.

Please Visit: www.westquoddy.com

Note: The Visitor Center is Open From Late May until Late September. And the Tower is Open to the Public Only on Limited days by the United States Coast Guard. Please Call or e-mail Visitors Center for more Information.

Light Keepers of the West Quoddy Lighthouse

Dates of Service

1st Keeper: Thomas Dexter 1808-1813
2nd Keeper: Peter Godfrey* 1813-39

Alfred Godfrey (Peter's son) 1839-42
Ebenezer Wormell 1840s-50s?
David Joy (assistant) c.1850s
William Coggins ? - 1856
William Godfrey 1856-60
Albert H. Godfrey (assistant) 1857-61
Richard Richardson 1860-61
Loring A. Leavitt (assistant) 1861-67
George A. Case 1861-77
Lowell Chase (assistant) 1867-78
Daniel Thayer 1877-79
Joseph Huckins (assistant) 1878-80
Henry M. Godfrey 1879-82
Garrison Crowell (assistant) 1880-82
William Fanning 1882-86
Walter B. Mowry (assistant) 1882-86
Alvin Eldrige (assistant) 1886-87
John Connors 1886-90
Henry M. Godfrey (assistant) 1887-89
George W. Sabin (assistant) 1889-90
John W. Guptill 1890-99
Irwin Young 1890-93
Edward L. Horn (assistant) 1893-95
Edwin L. Eaton (assistant) 1895-1900
Leonard Foster 1897+/-
Fred M. Robbins (assistant) 1900-1901
Ralph Temple Crowley 1900-15?
Warren A. Murch 1899-05
Ephraim N. Johnson (asst) 1901-05
Ephraim N. Johnson (head) 1905-31

Herbert Robinson (assistant) 1905-07
Eugene C. Ingalls (assistant 1907-12
Leo Allen (assistant) 1912-?
Ralph Temple Crowley (asst) ?-1915?
Arthur Robie Marston (asst) 1920s
Earle Ashby c. 1939-?

Eugene N. Larrabee c. 1930-40
Robert Howard Gray** 1934-1952
**The U.S. Coast Guard absorbed the Light House Service in 1939. "Bob" Gray was thus both the last Lighthouse Service keeper and the first Coast Guard keeper.

All subsequent individuals at West Quoddy Light Station were Coast Guard personnel:

Nelson Geel ?
Frank Mitchell ?
Almon Mitchell ?
Robert W. Brooks Early 50s
Hoyt Cheny c.1950
Don Ashby 1953-56
James Lewis ?
Nolan Snipes ?
Alexander Snedden 1949-52
Richard Kelley ?
Patrick Stevens 1957 – 1960
Vern Ryan BM3 1956-57
Paul Kessler EN1 1956
Leon Chiappini 1958-60
Jerry Preston Thomas 1958-62
John W. Willmott (engineer) 1959-61
David Hardman EN2 1960-61 (plus briefly 1956)
Russell Reilly BM1 1960-61
Howard Johnson SN 1960-61

Lamont VanWezemaal (relief) 1961-62

(Photo Below)

Stephen H. Rogers Dec '63
Bruce Keene 1962-64
John Wiley Grandey II 1963-64
Clayton L. Coffin June 1964 -
George Staples 1964-65
Robert Bran 1964-65
Richard Copeland 1965
Clayton L. Coffin 1966-68
Thomas Keene 1967
Robert Brann, Jr. 1966-67
Reuben Bryer 1968-69
Richard "Gary" Craig 1968-69
Clarence Fenton EN 3. 1970 – 71
David Pratt SN 2. 1970 – 71
David Melochick En 2. 1970 - 71
Clifton Scofield 1974-78
Robert Marston 1975
George "Bubba" Eaton 1978-82
Paul Latour 1980-81
Owen Gould 1982-84
John Richardson 1984-86

The last Coast Guard keeper at West Quoddy Head before its 1988 automation was Malcolm Rouse. Asked by the *Boston Globe* what he thought of automation, Rouse responded:

What I think you can't print. . . . It's the best duty a man can have for being with your family. I'm up when that sunshine hits here -- it's the first place it hits -- and oh, I'll miss that -- it sure is beautiful. It makes a pretty picture.

Today many visitors from all over the World enjoy the beauty of West Quoddy Lighthouse.

A chronological history of the United States Lighthouses:

This chronology of US lighthouse history is by no means intended to be all-inclusive. It is included to provide an understanding of the important role that lighthouses fulfilled over the years, some of the changes an management and methods that existed over time, and the important role played by the lighthouses.

1789 The ninth law passed by the newly created Congress of the United States, and the first to make provision for public work, created the Lighthouse Establishment as an administrative unit of the Federal Government. This bill provided "the necessary support, maintenance and repairs of all lighthouses, beacons, buoys and public piers erected, placed, or sunk before the passing of this act, at the entrance of, or within any bay, inlet, harbor, or port of the United States, for rendering the navigation thereof easy and safe, shall be defrayed out of the treasury of the United States."

1812 Parabolic reflectors were introduced in lighthouses. This lens was later discarded, and improved reflectors were imported."

1812 Congress authorized the Secretary of the Treasury to purchase Winslow Lewis' patent for a reflecting lantern, and to incorporate that lighting system in all US lighthouses.

An Act of Congress placed the construction of all lighthouses under the review of the Board of Navy Commissioners. E. and G. W. Blunt, publishers of Blunts "Coast Pilot," submitted a statement to the Secretary of the Treasury, in which they stated "the whole lighthouse system needs revision, a strict superintendence and an entirely different plan of operation."

1838 As a result of growing negative sentiments relative to lighthouse operation, Congress divided the Atlantic coast into six lighthouse districts, and the Great Lakes coast into two. A naval officer was detailed to each lighthouse district, a revenue cutter or a hired vessel was placed at his disposal, and he was instructed to inspect all aids to navigation, report on their conditions, and recommend future courses of action. After inspecting a number of lighthouses, naval officers submitted reports and recommendations, resulting in the deferral of 31 lighthouses for which appropriations had already been made.

Congress appropriated funds for importing two Fresnel lenses.

1841 The first imported Fresnel lens was installed in the Navesink Lighthouse.

1842 The House of Representatives passed a resolution requesting the Committee on Commerce to make an inquiry into the expenditures of the Lighthouse Establishment since 1816 to identify possible cost-cutting measures, and to evaluate alternate management systems.

The Committee on Commerce, as requested on 18 February 1842, made its report to Congress. It had found the operation and administration of the lighthouse work reasonably satisfactory, opposed the transfer of the Lighthouse Establishment to any other department, and recommended that permanent inspectors be appointed

The Secretary of the Treasury dispatched Navy Lieutenants Thornton A. Jenkins and Richard Bache to Europe to identify opportunities for improvement to the US lighthouse system. Subsequently, the Secretary submitted their report asking that a board be appointed to oversee lighthouse improvements. As was previously the case with similar recommendations, Congress did nothing!

1847 The Lighthouse Appropriation Bill of 1848 provided for "furnishing the lighthouses on the Atlantic coast with means of rendering assistance to shipwrecked mariners." This was the first appropriation by the national government for rendering assistance to the shipwrecked from shore bound facilities.

1851 Congress finally appointed a pro-tem board to investigate "the lighthouse problem." The board submitted a seven hundred and sixty page report, strongly recommending the creation of a Lighthouse Board to oversee the US lights.

1852 The Lighthouse Board, which would administer the lighthouse system until 1 July 1910, was organized. The Board was composed of two officers of the Navy, two officers of the Engineer Corps, and two civilians of "high scientific attainments." The Board was empowered under the Secretary of the Treasury, who served as President of the Board. The Board was further empowered to divide the coast of the United States into twelve lighthouse districts, with an army or navy officer assigned as lighthouse inspector for each.

1853 George G. Meade, then assigned to the Corps of Topographical Engineers and later commander of the Union forces at Gettysburg, invented a lamp adopted by Lighthouse Board.

By this date, only five lighthouses in the United States were equipped with Fresnel lens.

1855 The U. S. Lighthouse Service investigated the use of steam whistles as fog signals.

The Lighthouse Board made some unsuccessful experiments with various forms of petroleum as fuel for the lights...

1857 The schooners LAMPLIGHTER and WATCHFUL were purchased as the first Great Lakes lighthouse tenders

1859 Congress empowered the Lighthouse Board to determine when a lighthouse could be decommissioned, based on changes in commerce, alteration in channels, or other causes.

1859 By this date, Fresnel lenses had been installed in the vast majority of lighthouses in the United States.

1862 A bill to reorganize the Navy Department was introduced in the Senate, of which one of the proposed changes was the transfer of the Lighthouse Establishment to the Navy Department. Subsequently, the Chairman of the Lighthouse Board, himself a Navy Admiral, submitted a report expressing the Board's unanimous disapproval of the proposed change. In the end, the bill failed, and the Lighthouse Establishment remained under the Treasury Department.

1864 Lard oil was adopted within the Lighthouse Establishment as the standard illuminant, replacing colza, rapeseed and sperm oil.

1866 By this date, most of the lights that had become discontinued during the Civil War had been repaired and re-lighted

1867 Congress fixed the maximum pay of light keepers at $600.00, a law which remained unchanged for 50 years.

1874 Congress extended the jurisdiction of the Lighthouse Board over the Mississippi, Missouri, and Ohio Rivers.

Congress passed a law whereby it became a Federal offense for anyone to injure any pier, breakwater, or other work of the United States for the improvement of rivers, harbors, or navigation.

1877 Kerosene began to be used within the Lighthouse Establishment. Until this time, sperm oil, rapeseed, or lard oils were being used.

1880 Congress asserted that "masters of lighthouse tenders shall have police powers in matters pertaining to government property and smuggling."

1881 A first attempt at the use of oil gas lighted beacons was undertaken.

1884 The Lighthouse Board introduced a uniform for male lighthouse keepers, as well as for masters, mates, and engineers of lightships and tenders. Wearing of both dress and fatigue uniforms was also made mandatory.

1885 The Lighthouse Board reported that It had "at last succeeded in clothing all the male light-keepers, and the officers and crews of the lightships and the lighthouse tenders, in a neat, appropriate, and economical uniform, which the laborers employed as acting light-keepers are not allowed to wear. It is believed that "uniforming" the personnel of the service, some 1,600 in number, will aid in maintaining its discipline, increase its efficiency, raise its tone, and add to its esprit de corps."

Kerosene was adopted as the principal illuminant.

1886 Congress authorized an increase in the number of lighthouse districts within the Lighthouse establishment to 16.

The placement of an arc light in the torch of the Statue of Liberty, in New York Harbor, marks the first use of electricity for illuminating an aid to navigation in the US.

Officers and crews of lightships and lighthouse tenders became entitled to free treatment and care by the Public Health Service on the application of their commanding officers.

1887 Fourteen-Foot Bank became the first lighthouse in the US built on a caisson sunk in the sand bottom by the pneumatic process.

1892 The Lighthouse Service began being charged customs duties on certain articles of lighthouse supply not manufactured in the United States, previously imported duty free.

1896 President Grover Cleveland placed the U. S. Lighthouse Service within the Federal Civil Service

1898 An electric arc lamp was installed in the south tower of the Navesink lighthouse, making it the first primary lighthouse lighted by electricity, and the only shore station outfitted with its own generator.

1903 Congress transferred the Lighthouse Service from the Treasury Department to the newly formed Department of Commerce and Labor.

Compressed acetylene dissolved in acetone was first used at Jones Rocks Beacon in Connecticut, and South Hook Beacon in New Jersey.

1910 Congress abolished the Lighthouse Board and created the Bureau of Lighthouses to have complete charge of the Lighthouse Service. As a result, Mr. George R. Putnam and Mr. John S. Conway took office as the first

Commissioner of Lighthouses and first Deputy Commissioner of Lighthouses.

1911 A new type of oil-vapor lamp was developed which was believed to be an improvement on existing lamps. It reportedly provided greater candlepower per unit of oil used and practically superseded the carbonization of the oil, which has been a defect of previous types of oil-vapor lamps."

1912 As a result of the increasing cost of Fresnel lenses imported from France, the Lighthouse Service took steps to encourage American glass manufacturers in the production of lighthouse lenses.

A system of "efficiency stars and pennants," designed to promote efficiency and friendly rivalry among lighthouse keepers was initiated.

The Lighthouse Service installed a uniform system of inspection, introduced a new system of boat keeping and reporting, and revised the methods of keeping the general accounts in both the Bureau of Lighthouses and its district offices.

1914 The first Conference of Lighthouse Inspectors was held

1915 The use of the Canadian diaphone fog signal, manufactured by the Canadian Signal Company was first introduced in the United States

The installation of temporary unmanned gas lights for winter use at certain isolated stations on the Great Lakes was tried. This permitted the keepers to leave under safer conditions and at the same time giving service to late season mariners.

1916 Congress provided that "light keepers and assistant light keepers of the Lighthouse Service shall be entitled to medical relief without charge at hospitals and other stations of the Public Health Service under the rules and regulations governing the seamen of the merchant marine."

The Naval Appropriations Act provided for the mobilization of the Lighthouse Service in time of war by authorizing the President, "whenever in his judgment a sufficient national emergency exists, to transfer to the service and jurisdiction of the Navy Department, or of the War Department, such vessels, equipment, stations and personnel of the Lighthouse Service as he may deem to the best Interest of the country."

A device for automatically replacing burned-out incandescent electric lamps was developed and placed in use at several light stations

1917 Congress appropriated $300,000 to enable the U. S. Coast Guard to extend its telephone system to include all Coast Guard stations, and to include the most important light stations that then had no alternate means of rapid communication.

The first experimental radio beacon was set up, paving the way for later widespread use of radio in ship direction-finding.

1918 Congress changed the designation of Lighthouse Inspectors, who were in charge of the 19 lighthouse districts, to that of Superintendents of Lighthouses.

As part of a major cost-cutting move, the Lighthouse Service adopted the use of cotton towels in place of linen.

Congress provided retirement benefits for persons in the field service of the U. S. Lighthouse Service, including light keepers and lightship personnel.

1919 The Acting Secretary of the Treasury advised that light keepers and the officers and crews of vessels were not entitled to the benefits of the Public Health Service free of charge after retirement.

The Coast Guard had installed telephones at 139 light stations.

1920 Congress provided a system of general retirement for the civil employees of the U. S. Government, benefited those employees of the Lighthouse Service who were not covered by the retirement law of 20 June 1918.

A revision of the uniform regulations authorized light keepers and depot keepers to wear sleeve insignia to indicate length of service.

1921 system of pay increases for length of service was introduced as a means maintaining more efficient personnel on Lighthouse Service vessels.

1922 As a further cost cutting measure, acetylene lanterns, previously acquired from the manufacturers, began being made at the General Lighthouse Depot.

During Fiscal Year 1922, a readjustment was made of pay scales on vessels of the Lighthouse Service on the Atlantic and Pacific coasts and the Great Lakes and a system of longevity pay for all officers was introduced,

1925 Congress provided for disability retirement within the Lighthouse Service.

Congress authorized the purchase of rubber boots, oilskins, etc., for the use of personnel while engaged in lighthouse work requiring such equipment.

Congress repealed the law providing a ration allowance for keepers of lighthouses and increased their salaries correspondingly..

1926 Congress extended the benefits of the Public Health Service to apply to light keepers located at isolated points, who previously had been unable to avail themselves of such benefits.

1928 The first radio beacon in the United States, automatic in operation, was completed and placed into operation.

1930 Congress provided "that light keepers and vessel officers and crews, who during their active service were entitled to medical relief at hospitals and other stations of the Public Health Service, may be given such relief after retirement as Is now applicable to retired officers and men in other branches of the Government service, under joint regulations to be prescribed by the Secretary of the Treasury and the Secretary of Commerce."'

1932 The 2nd Lighthouse District completed an improved type of boat for delivering bulk kerosene between the tender and the light stations.

A photo-electric-controlled alarm system for checking the operation of an unwatched electric light was developed.

1935 After extensive testing, a system of flashing-light characteristics to indicate the purpose of buoys was placed in general operation.

1936 The Service's annual report for this year made the claim that the Lighthouse Service was perhaps the most decentralized agency of the Federal Government, with less than one percent of its 5,000 employees located at the seat of government,"

Lighthouse Service radio engineers designed and constructed improved radio beacon equipment, including new types of transmitters and transmitter exciters for modernizing older type radio beacons."

There were 1,644 more flashing lights than fixed lights in service, and the Lighthouse Service was continuing its policy of changing oil-burning fixed lights to occulting lights using acetylene or electric illuminant.

With the rapidly increasing network of highways, the Lighthouse Service began making increased use of truck for servicing its facilities.

The continued extension of commercial electric power lines even into the remoter sections of the United States had a reliable source of energy for the operation of signals at an increasing number of lighthouses.

1938 President Theodore Roosevelt enlarged substantially the number of "personnel in the Lighthouse Service who are subject to the principle of the civil service," which allowed advancement in the Service solely on individual merit.

The first low power, unattended "secondary" radio aid to navigation was established at St. Ignace, Michigan.

The program for the broadcasting of marine information by means of radiophones had been expanded to five additional radiophone broadcasting stations on the Great

Lakes, as well as such broadcasts from Key West and New Orleans.

The Lighthouse Service Radio Laboratory completed the developmental work on a high-power radio beacon amplifier, on ultrahigh frequency radiophone equipment, and on a calling unit to increase the efficiency and reliability of radiophone circuits.

The Lighthouse Service Radio Laboratory was moved from the shops of the lighthouse depot in Detroit, Michigan to the Lazaretto Lighthouse Depot in Baltimore, where a building had been constructed for its installation.

1939 The total personnel of the Service as of June 30, 1939, was 5,355, consisting of 4,119 full-time and 1,156 part-time employees, the former including 1,170 light keepers and assistants; 56 light attendants; 1,995 officers and crews of lightships and tenders; 113 Bureau officers, engineers, and draftsmen, and district superintendents and technical assistants; 226 clerks, messengers, janitors, and office laborers; 157 depot keepers and assistants, including watchmen and laborers; and 482 field-force employees engaged in construction and repair work."

The total number of aids to navigation maintained by the Lighthouse Service was 29,606, which represented an increase of 849 over the previous year."

Under the President's Reorganization Plan No. 11, the responsibilities of the Bureau of Lighthouses were transferred to the Coast Guard.

On July 7, the Lighthouse Bureau was officially eliminated, and its personnel moved themselves and their equipment to Coast Guard Headquarters. Thus lighthouses returned to the jurisdiction of the Treasury Department.

Suitable observance of the one hundred and fiftieth anniversary of the Lighthouse Service was called for by a joint resolution of Congress, and signed by the President on May 15. By this resolution the week of August 7, 1939, was designated lighthouse week.

The information above was paraphrased and condensed from "The U.S. Coast Guard Chronology and aids to Navigation and the United States Lighthouse Service."

Light Station Components:

The National Maritime Initiative adheres to the U.S. Lighthouse Service's 1915 definition of a lighthouse as being a light station where a resident keeper(s) was employed. The term "light station" refers to the tower as well as any supporting structures. Light stations initially consisted of the light tower, a dwelling, a garden site, a place to store oil, and maybe a chicken house and shelter for a milk cow. The increased complexity of operation, with the introduction of the more sophisticated Fresnel lens and fog signal in the 1850s, particularly the steam-operated ones, brought about a need for more personnel, which in turn required additional housing and other support buildings such as fog signal buildings, workshops, cisterns and water catchments basins, storage buildings, garages, radio buildings, boathouses and tramways, among others. By the 1920s and 1930s, however, the majority of light stations had electric service, reducing the number of staff necessary to operate the station. As ancillary buildings at many stations, especially shore stations, were rendered useless, the makeup of the light station began to change. In the 1960s, the automation of many light stations led to the surplus or demolition of many obsolete, yet historic, buildings.

Light tower:

The tower served principally as a support for the lantern which housed the light. The lantern was typically a round, square, octagonal, or decagonal-shaped cast-iron enclosure surrounded by an exterior stone or cast iron gallery with railing. Access to the lantern at the top of the tower was via stone, wood, or cast iron stairs which either wind around a central column or spiral along the interior sides of the tower walls (a few had straight sets of stairs which ran from landings around the tower interior). Windows in the tower were positioned to provide daylight onto the stairs. For taller towers, landings were provided at regular intervals. The top landing ended at the watch room where the keeper on duty ensured the optic was functioning properly. The lantern room above was usually reached via a ladder.

The most recognizable lighthouse type is the stand-alone tower such as Cape Hatteras Lighthouse. Lighthouses of this type come in many shapes including conical, square, octagonal, cylindrical, and even one triangular. Lighthouse towers may also be attached or integral to the keepers dwelling, and in a few cases, fog signal buildings. Attached towers are connected to a keepers quarters as a separate structure, often by a hyphen; whereas integral towers are those structurally built into the structure with the tower extending through the roof.

Lantern:

In the early days, lanterns were made of thin copper frames that held small panes of glass. The glass framing extended from the gallery deck to above the lighting equipment it held. A copper dome topped by a ventilator served as the roof of the lantern. Its design has given it the appearance of a bird cage, and in more recent years it has been known by that name. In addition to using small panes of glass that were of poor quality, these lanterns were generally not of adequate size to hold Fresnel lenses. Consequently, when the Fresnel lens was introduced in the 1850s, most of the old style lanterns were replaced with new lanterns designed to hold the larger and heavier Fresnel lenses. Today only a few of the old-style lanterns survive on lighthouses, including Prudence Island Lighthouse in Portsmouth, Rhode Island; Baileys Harbor Lighthouse, Lake Michigan; and Selkirk Lighthouse in Pulaski, New York.

There were four sizes of lanterns created to accommodate the seven standard sizes or orders of Fresnel lenses--a separate design for the first-, second-, and third-orders, and one design for the fourth- through sixth-order lenses. Made of cast iron plate, they were six-, eight-, and ten-sided lanterns, although round and square lanterns were sometimes used for range lights. They had large panes of glass, one pane to a side for the smaller lanterns, and as many as three panes (one over the other) per side for the two largest size lanterns. One of the metal panels was hinged to serve as a doorway providing access to the gallery or walkway on the exterior of the lantern.

In the late 19th century the helical bar lantern was introduced. Rather than having vertical astragals, they had diagonal ones. On the larger lanterns the astragals crossed. The lighthouse officials believed these types of lanterns gave off a brighter light when housing rotating lenses because the light beam was only partially blocked at any one time by the diagonal astragals versus a split second total eclipse of the light beam by vertical astragals.

<u>Keeper's dwelling</u>:

Second in importance to the light tower, dwellings for light keepers and their families were generally in the early days simple, 1 ½-story wooden or stone structures. Since lighthouses had only one keeper, there was only one dwelling. After 1852 with the coming of the Fresnel lens and the Lighthouse Board, more keepers began to be assigned to light stations, and, of course, it became necessary to have more living accommodations. Keeper's quarters could be single, double, triple, or even quadruple dwellings; they reflected the prevailing architectural styles, adaptations to geographical conditions, or regional tastes. Complaints by keepers concerning lack of privacy for their families finally persuaded the Lighthouse Board not to build tri-plex housing. By 1913 the U.S. Lighthouse Service stressed that "recent practice favors detached houses, insuring greater privacy, and giving better opportunity for yards and gardens."

For all practical purposes, prior to 1852 there were two types of land-based lighthouses--either a detached dwelling or an integral dwelling with the light tower rising out of the roof. The early integral towers had the tower supported by the roof system. As time went, the lighting apparatus grew heavier, particularly with the advent of the Fresnel lens, and the tower was supported from the foundation of the keeper's dwelling. In colder climates, such as New England and the Great Lakes, the light tower often was either attached to the dwelling or an enclosed passageway was built between the two structures.

Oil house:

During the early day's oil was often stored in the lighthouse. As late at the early 1850s, plans for the first west coast lighthouses called for the oil storage area to be in the basement. Some lighthouse towers were constructed with attached oil room and workroom structures which were generally one-story, constructed of masonry, had gable roofs, and were modest in detailing; examples include Pensacola, Pigeon Point, and Yaquina Head Lighthouses.

By 1890, all except a few lighthouses in the United States were using kerosene. The volatile nature of kerosene necessitated the construction of separate oil houses, which were usually built of fireproof materials such as brick, stone, iron plate and concrete. Congress issued a series of small appropriations for the construction of separate fireproof oil houses at each lighthouse station. Installation of these structures began in 1888 and completed about 1918. The 1902 Instructions to Light-Keepers stated: "All mineral oil belonging to the Light House Service shall be kept in an oil house or a room by itself. The oil house shall be visited daily to detect loss by leakage or otherwise, and every precaution taken for the safe keeping of the oil."

Though they varied in size, lighthouses with smaller lenses had relatively small oil houses and those stations with the large lenses had relatively larger oil houses. Constructed of stone, brick, cast iron, and concrete, oil houses were small, simple, and functional, usually with a gabled or a pyramid roof. When oil was no longer required, the structures were used for other storage purposes, often paint storage.

Fog signals building:

Fog signals were developed to assist mariners when fog obscured the light. Fog signals included bells, cannons, sirens, horns, and trumpets, and were usually housed in separate buildings, which were either attached to the light tower or free-standing. The equipment for large coastal stations was provided in duplicate to guard against breakdowns which might cause an interruption in fog signal operation.

Light stations began to get a little more complex with the introduction of a fog signals. The first fog signal was a cannon placed at Boston Harbor light in 1719. In the 1820s a bell fog signal was apparently introduced at West Quoddy Head Lighthouse in Maine. Subsequently other fog bell signals were added around New England and down to Chesapeake Bay; south of the bay fog occurs much less frequently.

In the very early days, fog bells were rung by striking the bell by hand; the bell installed at Pooles Island Lighthouse, Maryland, in the mid-1820s was operated by mechanical means, using a clockwork system. A tower on which the fog bell hung was built near the shore. A rope ran from a striker to the top of the tower where weights were attached. As those weights slowly fell they would activate the striker so that it struck the bell periodically. When the weights hit bottom after 45 minutes, sometimes an hour and a half and the keeper cranked the weights back to the top to start the process over again. Later, Daboll, Stevens, and Gamewell invented clockworks which were advertised as good for 10,000 blows of the fog bell with one winding. With a rapid characteristic, i.e., a blow every 10 seconds, a day could pass between windings; with a characteristic of a blow every 30 seconds, four days could pass before another winding. In time electricity was applied to fog signals which eased the burden of tending them. In the 1920s a device that turned the bell on automatically came into use. It was hygroscope measuring moisture in the air that activated the bell.

The earliest fog signal structures were wooden bell towers, later designs included iron construction. The towers were usually a tapering square shape topped by a pyramidal metal roof. The tower structure was often exposed except for the enclosed upper level area which protected the bell-striking mechanism. These towers were built in exposed marine environments and subjected to heavy vibrations from the striking of the bell. They had to be replaced frequently and few survive. For the most part, the ones that survive are metronome in shape.

On stations built offshore such as caisson and screw pile structures, the fog bell was usually mounted outside the top half-story of the dwelling (just below the lantern) and struck by machinery mounted on the inside. The striker hammer passed through a hole in the wall. In screw pile lighthouses the weights which drove the striking machinery were usually suspended by wire down through a wooden square shaft and/or in a closet. In many caisson lighthouses the weights were suspended by wire through a central hollow structural support column. The weights were usually suspended through the first level deck of a screw pile lighthouse or to the cellar level of a caisson lighthouse. When electric fog signal horns began to replace the fog bells, the new devices were often mounted on the deck of the lantern gallery, or in the case of a caisson lighthouse on the deck of the lower gallery, or in the case of a crib lighthouse on the crib foundation platform.

During the latter half of the 19th century the Lighthouse Board experimented with various types of fog signals, including whistles, trumpets, and sirens. At first whistles were not successful; mainly, the board later determined, because the tests were run on too small a steam whistle. Some years later it ran more tests, this time with the largest railroad steam whistle. The tests were successful and the steam whistle was installed at a number of light stations. These fog signals continued in service into the 20th century. A modified version of this signal continues in use, but operated by compressed air, not steam.

Daboll's trumpet was also experimented with, but it too apparently was not successful for it was not put into general use. This fog signal had a reed which was vibrated by compressed air and the sound came out of a large trumpet, one order measuring 17 feet long and 38 inches across the opening. The siren fog signal was first used in 1868 and was most successful.

Another fog signal used until recently, the diaphone, a Canadian development, gives off a two-tone sound that was made popular in the heyday of radio by a Lifebuoy soap advertisement. It was available in several sizes and used a single tone, two tone, and chime signal. These fog signals with their steam or compressed air apparatuses, switchboards, work benches, storage cupboards, generators, engines, air and water tanks, pumps, tools, and signal equipment occupied near barn-like buildings. The sound equipment was usually attached to the water side of the building. Built of masonry or wood, these structures were usually plain and highly functional, with the interiors being mostly open space until filled with concrete machinery mounts, tools, and equipment. Some fog signal buildings were built integral to the light tower. The Cape Arago Light Station and the octolateral brick stucco fog signal at Coquille River Light Station, Oregon, are examples. In a few cases, a fog signal station was established without a light.

Today fog signals, for the most part, are intended to aid small vessels and boats that do not have the advanced electronic gear such as radio direction finders, radar, sonar, and satellite guidance. As a result, the fog signal is being down-sized. The only fog signal the Coast Guard operates today is electronic horns: the ELG300 and ELG 500 which have a three to five mile range and the FA 232 have as ¼ to one mile range.

Radio beacon:

About 200 radio beacons located mostly at lighthouses, and formerly on lightships, were located on all ocean coasts and the Great Lakes. Commissioner George R. Putnam during his administration of aids to navigation put the evolving use of the radio as one of his proudest accomplishments; he considered the radio beacon the definitive guidance during fog for vessels that could afford radio direction finders. A vessel could search out a signal from a radio beacon and determine his position in relation to that station. This system is considered short range, effective between 10 and 175 miles. The equipment at the station consisted of antennas and transmitters and occupied space on the grounds and in a building. With the advent of new and better technology, the Coast Guard has taken all of their radio beacons out of service.

Storehouse:

Many onshore stations had separate frame or masonry storehouses were provisions, spare parts, and other items could be stored. Offshore stations made use of nearly every available space for storage. Caisson light stations used the cellars for storage of oil, coal, wood, provisions, and other items. Screw pile light stations usually had a wooden secondary landing built into the spider-like foundation below the first-level of the cottage. Here fuel, live animals, and other items could be stored. In times of storms, however, these areas were vulnerable to water damage. For all offshore stations, closets, the watch room, and the eaves under the upper half-story were used to store all kinds of materials.

Boat and boathouse:

In the early days the light keeper who tended an offshore lighthouse could justify a boat to go back and forth to the mainland. But if a keeper was responsible for a light on the mainland, he would have to have strong justification; no matter how isolated the lighthouse may be, to be successful in obtaining a locally-made boat from the government. These boats usually had a sail and could be rowed. At the lighthouse, these boats were pulled ashore when not in use and left in the open.

The Lighthouse Board was more generous in size and number of boats, partly because of increase in personnel. The Board also began providing boathouses to shelter the boats. The boathouses were simple gabled-roofed sheds with iron rails on which to pull the boat into the shed. Such structures became more important as technology advanced and the engine-powered boat came into use. These early boats were rather cranky and the engine would often stop running at inopportune times. Boats were supplied to offshore lighthouses such as the screw pile, caisson, wave swept, and crib types as well as the Florida reef lights. Occasionally, isolated shore light stations without road access received boats so keepers could travel to nearby towns. Two boats were usually assigned to each offshore station and they hung suspended from davits on opposite sides of the station, the keeper could maintain a lee for safer leaving and arriving, regardless of wind conditions. Protection from the weather was supplied by canvas covers.

There were several reasons for justifying two boats at an offshore light station, and one of them was the increase in rescues of fishers and boaters in trouble, and in some sections of the country, pilots of planes forced down in nearby waters. The engine-powered boats, which appeared soon after the turn of the century, could get to an accident quicker. One cannot but be impressed with the number of rescues by keepers that were recorded in the Lighthouse Service Bulletin, the internal newsletter of the Lighthouse Service.

Barn and garage:

Some of the light stations received government-built barns where horses and perhaps a cow could be sheltered. With the coming of the automobile, light stations began to include garages. These structures were simple, standard garage structures with up to three bays. Many barns were converted to garages including Pensacola Light Station, Florida, and Montauk Point Light Station, New York. The resourcefulness of lighthouse personnel is illustrated by the 1950s conversion of a garage into living quarters at Cove Point Light Station, Maryland. The garage had been moved and remodeled into a dwelling.

Privy:

The necessary houses for shore stations were generally no different than any other privy. Usually they were simple wooden frame structures, but on occasion they could be fancy, following the style of the dwelling. Currituck Light Station had one that was of Queen Anne design to match the keeper's quarters. Some were made of brick, a material not used for privately constructed privies.

For offshore stations, the privy was usually constructed so it cantilevered over the lower exterior gallery rail. The privy hole dropped directly into the water. They were small, accommodating only one user at a time. Those at screw pile lighthouses were made of wood, while the ones at caisson lighthouses were made of iron plate. On the latter, the privy was sometimes used as part of the electrical grounding system. A metal cable ran from the lightning rod down the roof of the lantern, then from the roof of the dwelling to the top of the privy which was attached to the iron- plated caisson tube. With more stringent environmental laws and newer technology, indoor plumbing came to land-based light stations. By the 1970s offshore light stations began to convert interior spaces for restrooms. Holding tanks and electric commodes were used. The former privy was sometimes converted for storage or paint locker. With the erection of the Texas tower type lighthouses indoor plumbing became standard.

Water collection system:

All lighthouses needed water. Some stations used wells. At other stations water was piped in from nearby springs. Often, water collection systems provided water for drinking, washing, and for steam-powered fog signals. Rain water was often collected from the roof of light station structures channeling the water from gutters and downspouts to pipes going to the water reservoirs. Rain water was usually not collected immediately; rather, the rain was allowed to fall for a while uncollected so the roof would be washed. Periodically the roofs were cleaned by manual means. At other light stations, particularly in drier regions such as California, water was not only caught by roof runoff but by large catch basins connected to storage cisterns and tanks were used to trap the rainwater. These catch basins were generally constructed of brick, later covered with cement or made only of cement. The Old Point Loma Lighthouse in San Diego still has the remains of its old brick-lined underground cistern which held 10,000 gallons. Its 2800 square-foot catch-basin was attached to it. Other examples of existing catch-basins are found at Point Reyes, San Luis Obispo and East Brothers Light Stations, all in California.

Where the underground water level was too high, a light station may have wooden water storage tanks aboveground. The water system for the Anacapa Island Light Station off southern California consists of a 30,000-square-foot concrete rain catchments basin and two round 50,000-gallon redwood tanks housed in a specially built water tank building. As the average rainfall is only eight inches providing only 18,000 gallons of water a year, lighthouse tenders supplied the additional water which was pumped into the storage tanks.

At offshore stations such as screw pile and caisson stations the gutters and downspouts were attached to a water collection system inside the structure. In screw pile structures the system was connected to water tanks, usually one in each of three or four rooms of the first-floor of the cottage. The tanks were made either of cypress or metal. A spigot at the base of each tank was positioned over a metal funnel cut into the floor so that any dripping or overflow could be controlled without flooding the cottage floors. These funnels are still intact in the Thomas Point Shoals Light Station, Maryland.

In the caisson light stations the cisterns were constructed into the concrete fill of the caisson cylinder just below the cellar level. There were usually two cisterns for each caisson light station. Like, the screw pile structures, the cisterns were connected to the downspouts. A hand pump in the kitchen, connected to the cellar cistern provided water to the kitchen sink. In times of drought buoy tenders would provide freshwater to top off the cisterns and other station water storage tanks.

Tramway:

A number of light stations had tramway tracks running from landings to the light station. The tramways were principally used to unload supplies and equipment from the lighthouse tender. A few of the tracks survive at a number of light stations, including Point Reyes, California, and Split Rock, Minnesota.

Lighthouse Depot:

From the beginning of the service, lighthouses had to be supplied with oil, wicks, extra chimneys for lamps, glass panes for the lantern and other equipment and materials such as brushes, brooms, oil containers, Lucerne's, clocks, dust pans, feather dusters, cleaning liquids and solids, paint, wick trimmers all required to keep these aids to navigation in operation. Fresnel lenses were more complex and with their installation came a substantial increase in required tools and equipment. As the lighthouse service grew, the number of lighthouse depots increased. A tender assigned to each district inspector supplied the light stations, placed and replaced lightships, and positioned and replaced buoys and demarks. In addition an inspector would arrive by a tender for his white glove inspection of the light station.

Lighthouse depots came into use in the midst of the Civil War with one per district. At the general depot on Staten Island, oil and lamps and other equipment were tested and often developed. All depots purchased supplies, including oil, and dispersed them to the districts. Those supplies destined for the east and Gulf coasts went largely by water, while those going to the Great Lakes and the west coast districts went largely by rail. Surviving examples of lighthouse depots include Staten Island Depot, New York (the first and general depot for the service); Detroit Depot, Michigan; and St. Josephs Depot, Michigan.

Some light stations also were used as buoy depots. Point Lookout Light Station, Maryland, became a buoy depot in 1883. Extant structures from the depot include a former coal shed (1884) used to resupply tenders, a buoy repair shed (1883), and remnants of the wharf piles and the concrete shore apron of the former rail delivery system.

Miscellaneous Structures:

Other typical station outbuildings might include piers, smokehouses, wood and coal sheds, and carpenters and blacksmiths workshops. Relatively newer station buildings exist at some light stations such as signal/radio beacon/generator buildings.

Sources: Excerpted from draft National Register of Historic Places Multiple Property Documentation form for "Light Stations of the United States;" George R. Putnam, Lighthouses and Lightships of the The Visitors Center in Most open Lighthouse in United States (Boston and New York: Houghlin Mifflin Co., 1917);The USCG history Department and R. Holland, America's Lighthouses: An Illustrated History (New York: Dover Publications, 1981 reprint) Deb Bridges, Junia Olson , Rangers Mr. Smith & Mr. Moores, West Quoddy Visitors Center in Lubec, Maine.

If you have more Information not listed in this Booklet about the Keepers. I would like to include in next Publishing. Currently I am looking for any Birth & Death dates at West Quoddy. We welcome your comments and suggestions. Please contact Carolyn @ CarolynM@usa.com

All rights reserved. No part of this Booklet may be reproduced in any form, or by any electronic or mechanical means, including information storage and retrieval systems, without permission in writing from Carolyn la MacMillan, Pembroke Maine Art, Pembroke Life in Photos

Photograph Credits: Pembroke Maine Art

Thank you and God Bless

C. la Macmillan

Notes

Notes

Notes

Notes

Notes

Made in the USA
Monee, IL
14 February 2023